Zebras

DISCOVER PICTURES AND FACTS ABOUT ZEBRAS FOR KIDS!

You've probably seen zebras at the zoo, but here are very cool facts about these creatures

Zebras actually are super close in relationship to horses and donkeys. How cool

Every single zebra has a unique pattern, so no two patterns are the same, and there are different reasons why the might have these stripes

All Zebras live in Africa in the wild, but many live in zoos all around the world

The pedestrian crossings that you see, are actually named based off the black and white stripes of zebras. Think about that next time you cross the street

You can ride a zebra, but they're smaller than horses and won't be able to old most adult humans

Zebras actually are pretty aggressive, and they have been known to kick other zebras to death and will bite humans if they get too close.

There are accounts of zebras actually killing lions. How's that for a predator

Zebras actually make similar sounds to horses, and they'll even growl and squeal

They can run over 63 kilometers an hour when they gallop around the plains, which is just fast enough to outrun some other predators

The foals of a litter can run with a herd within just a few hours of birth

Zebras are cool creatures, and here you learned some cool facts about them.

CPSIA information can be obtained
at www.ICGtesting.com
Printed in the USA
LVHW061703300122
709774LV00009B/640

9 781071 706138